I0164941

INTERFAITH INSPIRATION
Adult Coloring Book

Stress relieving designs

Contains inspirational quotes & illustrations

By Zarin June Buckingham

ISBN 978-0-9994351-3-7

Introduction

Coloring has become increasingly popular with adults in the United States and in other countries. People are coloring alone, with friends, in organized groups, and in library meetings. More than 15 million coloring books were sold in the US in 2015 according to an article in the Washington Post. Coloring can become a type of group therapy in social groups. It also seems to trigger a meditative response with decreased stress. Coloring involves three key components of stress reduction: repetition, pattern and detail. It brings people into the now and allows them to let go of any negative thoughts or anxiety by focusing them on the process of coloring. This response may only require 15 minutes of coloring per day and need not take up a large amount of time. Coloring allows people to be creative without requiring a specialized skill or talent. Also called 'mindfulness art', this activity also pulls people away from the ever-present computer and cell phone screens. Participating in a coloring group has been compared to going to a yoga or meditation class. It has even been used to reduce stress in patients undergoing treatment for cancer and compares favorably with group therapy. This is more than a trend; it may be good for you.

There are many ways to color these pictures. Various artistic media can be used (colored pencils, gel pens, etc.). Some like to focus on completing a picture in a given time frame, while others prefer to strive for perfection and take more time. After pictures are completed, they can be used as gifts or for home decoration.

The pictures in this book are organized around a theme and highlight the harmony and areas of agreement between religions and philosophies. The great faith traditions hold many of the same values. These include reverence for the Creator, respect for human life, and appreciation of the beauty of nature. Also, all faiths promote the development of human virtues, including trustworthiness, kindness, love, discipline, service, and humility. Despite these common values, differences can sometimes cause suspicion and animosity and commonalities go unnoticed. Reconciliation can only be based on mutual understanding.

Rest
in the
Lord
and wait
patiently for
HIM
Psalms 37:7

As you walk, eat, and travel,
be where you are.
Otherwise, you will miss most of your life.
. . . Buddha . . .

And ye shall know the truth,
and the truth shall
make you free.

...John 8:32...

I have been a stranger in a strange land.

Exodus 2:22

Possess a pure, kindly and radiant heart, that thine may be a sovereignty ancient, imperishable and everlasting.

-Baha'u'llah

Tell me and
I forget.
Teach me and
I remember.
Involve me and
I learn.

Benjamin Franklin

♡

When I do good, I feel good.
When I do bad, I feel bad. That's my religion.
... Abraham Lincoln ...

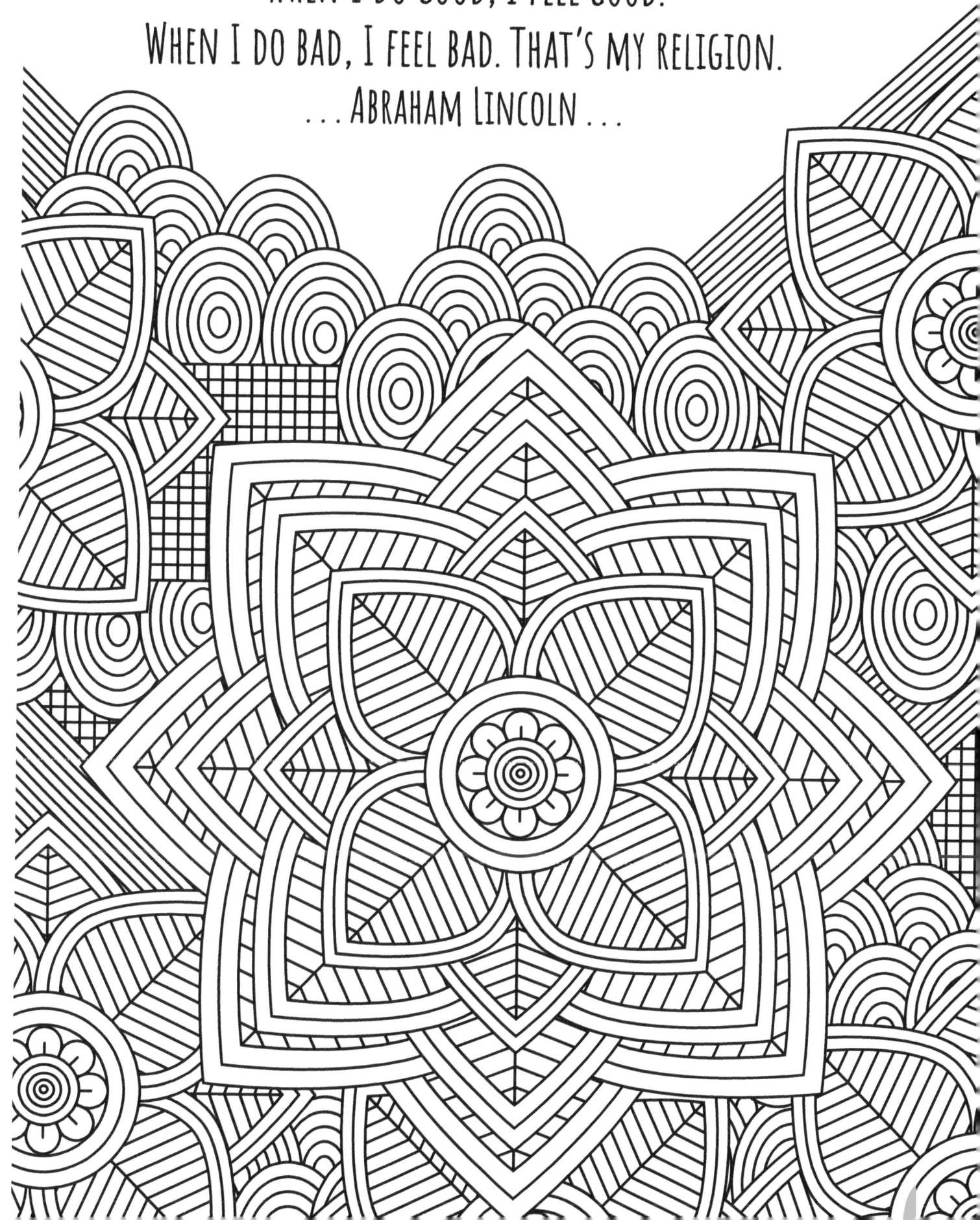

I offer you peace.
I offer you love.
I offer you friendship.
I see your beauty.
I hear your need.
I feel your feelings.
My wisdom flows from the highest source.
I salute that source in you.
Let us work together for unity and love.

~Gandhi

All religions - all this singing, is one song. The differences are just illusion and vanity.

The sun's light looks a little different on this wall than it does on that wall, and a lot different on this other one, but it's still

One Light

Rumi

O you who believe!

Avoid much suspicion,
indeed some suspicions are sins.
And spy not, neither backbite one another.

Koran 49:12

SPEAK JUSTICE

~KORAN 6:152

O Son of
Man!
Breathe not the sins of
others so long as thou art
thyself a sinner. Shouldst
thou transgress this
command, accursed wouldst
thou be, and to this
I bear witness.

~Baha'u'llah

Peace among religions is a precondition for world peace.

- Swami Agnivesh

Lord, make me an instrument of your
peace:
where there is hatred, let me sow love:
where there is injury, pardon;
where there is doubt, faith;
where there is despair, hope;
where there is darkness, light;
and where there is sadness, joy.

~Saint Francis of Assisi

If you don't know
where you are going,
any road
will get you
there.

Krishna

There are hundreds of ways
to kneel and kiss the ground.

Rumi

The earth is but one country,
and mankind its citizens.

Baha'u'llah

Is there any
reward for good
other than
good?

Koran 55:60

You must accept the truth
from whatever source it comes.
. . . Maimonides . . .

An eye for an eye
only ends up making the whole world blind.
. . . Gandhi . . .

God does not burden a soul
beyond that it can bear.
... Koran 2:286 ...

Be faithful
in small things because
it is in them that your strength lies.
. . . Mother Teresa . . .

The mind is
everything.

What you think
you become.

~Buddha

Do not impose on others
what you yourself do not desire.

. . . Confucius . . .

Our prayers

should be for blessings in general,

for God knows best

what is good for us.

. . . Socrates . . .

All who call on God in true faith,

earnestly from the heart,

will certainly be heard,

and will receive

what they have asked and desired.

. . . Martin Luther . . .

To one who has faith,
no explanation is necessary.
To one without faith,
no explanation is possible.

. . . St. Thomas Aquinas . . .

List of quotes and authors

Rest in the Lord and wait patiently for Him
Psalms 37:7

•••

As you walk, eat, and travel, be where you are.
Otherwise, you will miss most of your life.
Buddha

•••

And ye shall know the truth, and the truth shall make you free.
John 8:32

•••

I have been a stranger in a strange land.
Exodus 2:22

•••

Possess a pure, kindly and radiant heart, that thine may be a
sovereignty ancient, imperishable and everlasting.
Baha'u'llah
Hidden Words of Baha'u'llah, US Bahá'í Publishing Trust, 1985, p. 3

Tell me and I forget. Teach me and I remember. Involve me and I learn.
Benjamin Franklin

●●●

When I do good, I feel good.   When I do bad, I feel bad. That's my religion.
Abraham Lincoln

●●●

I offer you peace.
I offer you love.
I offer you friendship.
I see your beauty.
I hear your need.
I feel your feelings.
My wisdom flows from the highest source.
I salute that source in you.
Let us work together for unity and love.
Gandhi

●●●

All religions – all this singing, is one song.
The differences are just illusion and vanity.
The sun's light looks a little different on this wall than it does on that wall,
and a lot different on this other one, but it's still one light.
Jalaluddin Rumi

O you who believe! Avoid much suspicion, indeed some suspicions are sins.
And spy not, neither backbite one another.
Koran 49:12

●●●

Speak justice.
Koran 6:152

●●●

O Son of Man! Breathe not the sins of others so long as thou art thyself
a sinner. Shouldst thou transgress this command, accursed wouldst thou
be, and to this I bear witness.
Baha'u'llah
Hidden Words of Baha'u'llah, US Bahá'í Publishing Trust, 1985, p. 10

●●●

Peace among religions is a precondition for world peace.
Swami Agnivesh

●●●

Lord, make me an instrument of your peace: where there is hatred, let me sow
love: where there is injury, pardon; where there is doubt, faith; where there is
despair, hope; where there is darkness, light; and where there is sadness, joy.
Saint Francis of Assisi

If you don't know where you are going, any road will get you there.
Krishna

Origin not clear, but quote is attributed to Krishna.

● ● ●

There are hundreds of ways to kneel and kiss the ground.
Jalaluddin Rumi

● ● ●

The earth is but one country, and mankind its citizens.
Baha'u'llah

Gleanings from the Writings of Baha'u'llah p. 250

● ● ●

Is there any reward for good other than good?
Koran 55:60

● ● ●

You must accept the truth from whatever source it comes.
Maimonides

Foreword to The Eight Chapters Of Maimonides On Ethics, translated by
Joseph I. Gorfinkle, Ph.D. Columbia University Press, New York (1912). Page 35-36.

An eye for an eye only ends up making the whole world blind.
Attributed to Gandhi

●●●

God does not burden a soul beyond what it can bear.
Koran 2:286

●●●

Be faithful in small things because it is in them that your strength lies.
Mother Teresa
"The writings of Mother Teresa of Calcutta © by the Mother Teresa Center, exclusive licensee throughout the world of the Missionaries of Charity for the works of Mother Teresa. Used with permission. "

●●●

The mind is everything. What you think you become.
Atrributed to Buddha

●●●

Do not impose on others what you yourself do not desire.
Confucius
The Analects of Confucius

Our prayers should be for blessings in general, for
God knows best what is good for us.
Attributed to Socrates

● ● ●

All who call on God in true faith, earnestly from the heart, will certainly be
heard, and will receive what they have asked and desired.
Martin Luther

● ● ●

To one who has faith, no explanation is necessary. To one without faith, no explanation is possible.
St. Thomas Aquinas